World of Whales

Sperm Whales

by Katie Chanez

Bullfrog Books

Ideas for Parents and Teachers

Bullfrog Books let children practice reading informational text at the earliest reading levels. Repetition, familiar words, and photo labels support early readers.

Before Reading
- Discuss the cover photo. What does it tell them?
- Look at the picture glossary together. Read and discuss the words.

Read the Book
- "Walk" through the book and look at the photos. Let the child ask questions. Point out the photo labels.
- Read the book to the child, or have him or her read independently.

After Reading
- Prompt the child to think more. Ask: Some sperm whales live in pods. Can you name other animals that live in groups?

Bullfrog Books are published by Jump!
5357 Penn Avenue South
Minneapolis, MN 55419
www.jumplibrary.com

Copyright © 2024 Jump! International copyright reserved in all countries. No part of this book may be reproduced in any form without written permission from the publisher.

Library of Congress Cataloging-in-Publication Data

Names: Chanez, Katie, author.
Title: Sperm whales / by Katie Chanez.
Description: Minneapolis, MN: Jump!, Inc., [2024]
Series: World of whales | Includes index.
Audience: Ages 5–8
Identifiers: LCCN 2022051956 (print)
LCCN 2022051957 (ebook)
ISBN 9798885246019 (hardcover)
ISBN 9798885246026 (paperback)
ISBN 9798885246033 (ebook)
Subjects: LCSH: Sperm whale—Juvenile literature.
Classification: LCC QL737.C435 C43 2024 (print)
LCC QL737.C435 (ebook)
DDC 599.5/47—dc23/eng/20221031
LC record available at https://lccn.loc.gov/2022051956
LC ebook record available at https://lccn.loc.gov/2022051957

Editor: Eliza Leahy
Designer: Emma Almgren-Bersie

Photo Credits: Martin Prochazkacz/Shutterstock, cover, 6–7, 10, 14, 24; wildestanimal/Shutterstock, 1, 18–19, 23bl; Kjersti Joergensen/Shutterstock, 3; Roland Seitre/Minden Pictures/SuperStock, 4; Focus_on_Nature/iStock, 5; duncan1890/iStock, 8–9; agefotostock/Alamy, 9; THIERRY EIDENWEIL/iStock, 11; Andrea Izzotti/Shutterstock, 12–13, 23tl; 24fps/Shutterstock, 15, 23br; Blue Planet Archive/Alamy, 16–17, 23tr; Nature Picture Library/Alamy, 20–21.

Printed in the United States of America at Corporate Graphics in North Mankato, Minnesota.

Table of Contents

Hello, Whale!	4
Parts of a Sperm Whale	22
Picture Glossary	23
Index	24
To Learn More	24

Hello, Whale!

A sperm whale jumps.

Splash!

The whale has a big jaw.
It has big teeth.
Its head is square.
There is oil in it.

People used to hunt sperm whales.

Why?

They wanted the oil.

They used it to light lamps.

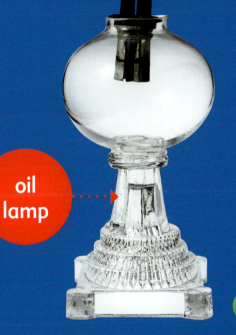

oil lamp

Sperm whales are dark gray.

They live in the ocean.
They use small fins to swim.

fin

They breathe air.
Each has a blowhole.

They dive.

This one goes one mile (1.6 kilometers) deep!

Why?

It chases squid.
It eats fish, too.

squid

calf

This mom had a baby.
It is called a calf.

It grows up in the pod.

The whales talk to each other.

How?

They make clicks.

Hello, whale!

Parts of a Sperm Whale

Sperm whales can be up to 60 feet (18 meters) long. That is almost as long as two school buses! Take a look at the parts of a sperm whale.

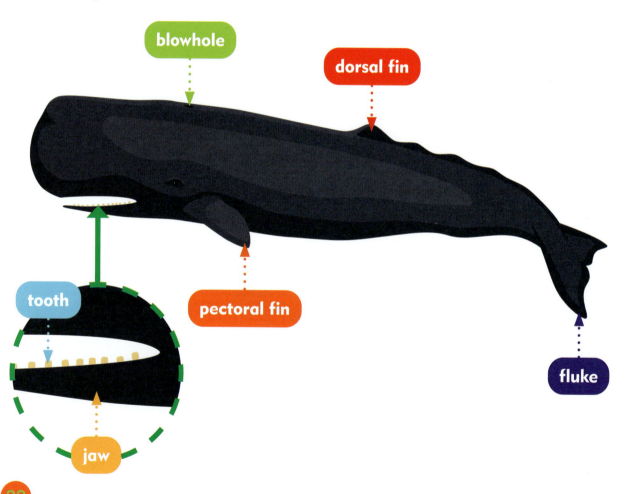

Picture Glossary

blowhole
A nostril on top of a whale's or dolphin's head used for breathing.

calf
A young whale.

pod
A group of whales.

squid
Sea creatures with long, soft bodies, eight arms, and two tentacles.

Index

blowhole 12
calf 17
clicks 20
dive 14
fins 11
hunt 9
jaw 6
ocean 11
oil 6, 9
pod 18
swim 11
teeth 6

To Learn More

Finding more information is as easy as 1, 2, 3.

❶ Go to www.factsurfer.com

❷ Enter "spermwhales" into the search box.

❸ Choose your book to see a list of websites.